Volume 9

LEGENDARY PERFORMERS

Nat "King" Cole

UNFORGETTABLE

Editor: Carol Cuellar
Produced by: Ivan Mogull

NAT "KING" COLE

It was the year 1937. In America, the hopes of everyone were rooted in the word "recovery." But if the depression seemed to be nearing an end for most of the nation, it had only deepened early that year for the wandering minstrels of a road show with the peculiarly fitting title "Shuffle Along."

The revue had shuffled all the way from Chicago to Long Beach, California, when an employee with obviously scant optimism for the show's future resigned without notice. More than that, he helped himself to the company's entire bankroll, $800.00, as his severance pay. "Shuffle Along" ground to a dead stop right there —and disintegrated.

Being broke and stranded in a strange town is never a pleasure to anyone. To one member of the company, its 18-year-old bandleader, Nathaniel Adams Coles, it was akin to a major calamity. Not only was he a rookie in show business, but he was very reluctant to write home for money since his father, the Rev. Edward Coles, a Baptist minister in Chicago, was considerably less than enthusiastic over having his children trotting around the country tooting horns and plunking pianos.

Young Nat wisely decided to make the best of his bad bargain and rough it out in California — at least until he could raise enough money to home with his head held high.

For the next several months he pounded beer-soaked Baldwins and Scotch-stained Steinways in dives from Bakerfield to San Diego. His asking price was five bucks a night, but he could be had for less, and usually was.

During that year one thing happened to the lanky, good-natured youngster. He abbreviated his name to Nat Cole, and one night while he was working in the old Los Angeles Century Club, a gagster slipped a paper crown on his head and dubbed him "King." From that night forward, he was to be Nat "King" Cole.

From the fold-up of "Shuffle Along," his life was punctuated with setbacks that turned out to be breaks. Some of them were large enough to provide him with footholds in his climb to the top of one of the toughest heaps in the world.

His singing was perhaps the most outstanding example. One of Cole's stops on his job-hunting rounds as an itinerant pianist was a Hollywood nightclub, the Swanee Inn. Their manager offered to pay Cole $75 a week if he could come up with a quartet overnight. At the time, for that kind of money, Nat would have produced the Philadelphia Symphony — or at least tried. He rushed out and corralled guitarist Oscar Moore, bass player Wesley Prince and a drummer whose name remains unrecorded because he failed to show up for work on opening night.

The trio was hardly an immediate sensation. That was the era of the big bands. Club owners demanded plenty of bodies and plenty of noise for their money. An instrumental trio — the group was strictly voiceless — was about as marketable as a vaudeville juggling act. Still, the "King" Cole Swingsters, as they were known then, did begin attracting the attention of jazz aficionados, attracted by the trio's musical purity. In time, club bookers

The Story...

became aware that these fans, small in number and strange in tastes though they might be, were willing to put their money where their loyalty was. When that understanding got around, Cole and his cohorts found that they were working with encouraging regularity. Sometimes their leader's take-home pay ran as high as $25 a week.

. . . It was during this cushy engagement at the Swanee Inn in Los Angeles, that Cole suffered another humiliating setback — or so, at least, it seemed to him at the time. One of those inevitable lushes in the audience, who wouldn't have known a dissonant chord from a harpsichord and wouldn't have cared, came stumbling to the bandstand and demanded that Nat sing his favorite tune "Sweet Lorraine."

Nat was gentle. "We don't sing," he said softly.

The portly patron was in no mood to be put off, however. He brought his eyes to focus on Cole and in the voice of a platoon sergeant commanded, "Sing!" That brought the manager of the place on the double. He summed up the situation on his mental cash register and gave Cole the word: "Sing. This guy's a big spender. Sometimes three bucks a night."

Nat Cole sang, nervously, reluctantly and, although there were no critics around at the time to comment on his performance, probably not very well. That voice was to become among the best-known in the world of popular music.

If Nat Cole's success story followed the Hollywood film formula, that first timorous rendition of Sweet Lorraine" would have been the climax. But it wasn't. The truth is that Cole wasn't then particularly impressed with his voice, although in the years since then critics have graced it with such terms as "pussy-willow textured."

And so he submerged himself again in the trio, which prospered increasingly as its cult of followers swelled. The bookings were progressively better until the group reached the once famous Trocadero, where a room was named for it.

With that sort of encouragement, the next logical step was a nation-wide tour. It was logical, but it wasn't especially successful. The trio's lukewarm reception was made worse when bass player Prince was drafted into the Army. Cole's return to the kindlier atmosphere of Los Angeles was anything but triumphant.

Meantime, however, Glenn Wallichs, a music store owner whom Cole had met while playing at the Radio Room next door, had teamed with songwriter Johnny Mercer and formed a new recording company — Liberty Records, later to become Capitol.

The company struggled through its first year and, in 1943, Wallichs heard Cole and his reorganized trio play "Straighten Up And Fly Right," a tune Nat had written during his lean years and sold for $50 to pay the rent. On the strength of it, Wallichs offered Cole a contract to record that song and do some other solo singing. That last part didn't appeal to Nat much, but he agreed. "Straighten Up And Fly Right," of course, was the first of his — and Capitol's — smash hits.

Still, Cole considered himself a full-time instrumentalist and a part-time singer. In the next three years, he and the trio made a number of records which today are regarded as collectors' items by jazz buffs, who rank Cole among the finest jazz pianists of all time.

So great was their reverence for him, in fact, that when he decided in 1946 to stake his future on his voice, instead of his fingers, some of his fans screamed with outrage that he was "selling out."

But Cole had set his course, a risky one but one he was determined to follow. For every jazz devotee who had listened raptly to his pianistics, hundreds of new followers were waiting just to hear his unique, breathy singing. As a single attraction in nightclubs and on records, he made more money than he had dreamed possible before.

And in 1947, in a $20,000 wedding, the second largest in Harlem history, Cole married Maria Ellington, a pretty band vocalist, who was more than willing to abandon her own career to become "King" Cole's queen. While they were honeymooning in Mexico, Nat received a call from a very close friend, music publisher, Ivan Mogull, stating that Nat's latest recording, the strange, haunting "Nature Boy" was another smash hit. The world was a bright place, indeed, for Nat Cole.

His tenure on Cloud Nine was characteristically brief. Cole still had a lot to learn — and quite a few things to teach.

Nat became aware that the Internal Revenue Service made a claim on back taxes, at which time Nat resolved this matter. With sudden luck smiling at him, he had one hit after another, which enabled him to pay off the IRS within two years.

In 1953, all the long smouldering worries, frustrations and resentments erupted within him, and he collapsed in the wings of Carnegie Hall during an Easter recital. The diagnosis was acute ulcers and internal hemorrhaging. Immediate surgery was recommended and performed with satisfactory results.

Since that brush with tragedy, Nat Cole became more taciturn, more introspective and less easy to lean on. He learned to invest his money — and built an efficiently operating organization around himself that allowed him a more reasonable amount of time for the things he loved most — his wife, their children, Carol, Natalie, Nat Kelly, Casey and Timolin, and baseball, to which he was hopelessly addicted.

No amount of planning, however, can stave off all defeats, especially for a man as willing to gamble as Nat Cole. And so he had his fair share of them, perhaps even more, to go with his incredibly indestructible success as a nightclub and recording artist.

Probably the bitterest of them, to Cole, was what happened to his network television show in 1957. Actually, the show was on the air for 64 weeks and could have remained if Cole had submitted to an airtime change insisted upon by NBC. But it didn't accomplish what Nat had hoped for and sacrificed for. It was a costly venture. Besides plowing part of his own salary back into the production costs, he turned down $500,000 worth of nightclub dates to stick with it.

Why did it mean so much to him? Although Cole never had been a shouting crusader for black rights, in his own quiet way he had always espoused the cause of racial equality, often more effectively than its more militant adherents. As the first black ever to have his own weekly show on TV, to him fell the opportunity, and the burden, of proving that such a program could achieve public acceptance on both sides of the Mason-Dixon Line.

Cole proved that. His show had good ratings and drew excellent reviews. The biggest "names" in show business guest-starred on it. But one of the peculiar details of the electronic medium defeated him. No national sponsor dared back Cole's play. In some areas, the program was sponsored regionally and successfully by the tab payers, but the big spenders of Madison Avenue, without whose support the show could not long survive, looked the other way.

His record of accomplishment over set-backs and disappointments is one that anyone would be proud to claim. For such a record to belong to the Alabama-born son of a minister who might never have sung at all if a slicker had not absconded with $800 and a nightclub drunk had not insisted on hearing someone wail "Sweet Lorraine," it might be classified as a minor miracle.

Nat "King" Cole became one of the hottest selling artists through the forties, fifties, and sixties. He became a legend with his fantastic sound. On December 7th, 1964, he suddenly took ill and he entered St. James Hospital in Santa Monica, California, where he was diagnosed as having lung cancer. On January 25, 1965, his left lung was removed. His sky rocketing career ended with his death on February 15, 1965.

Included in this collection are most all of the great standards which have become associated with Nat "King" Cole. We hope you enjoy playing and singing them, as they are a lasting tribute to one of the greatest performers of all time.

WHEN I FALL IN LOVE

Words by
EDWARD HEYMAN

Music by
VICTOR YOUNG

When I Fall In Love - 3 - 1

CHORUS

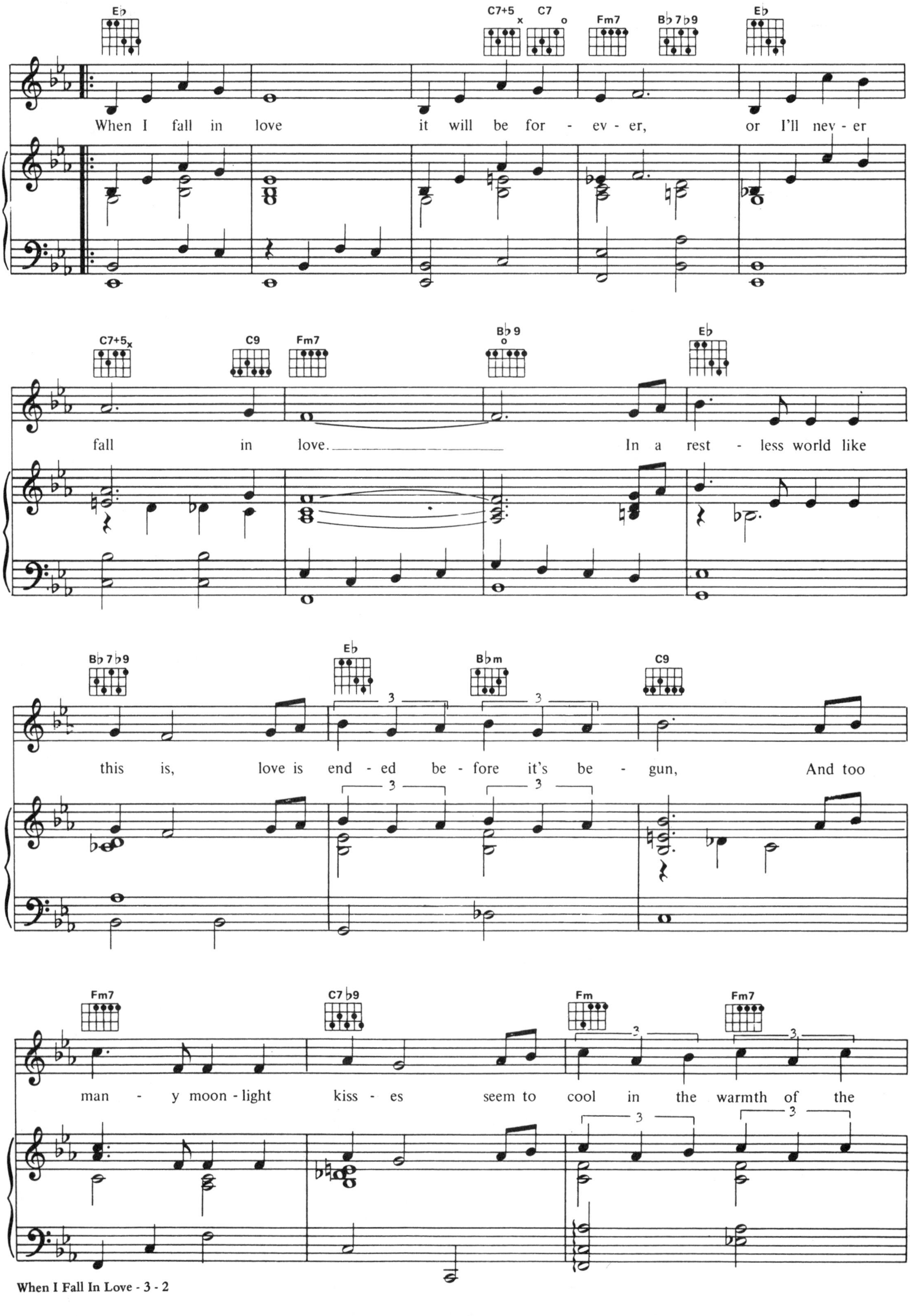

E♭ C7+5 C7 Fm7 B♭7♭9 E♭

When I fall in love it will be for - ev - er, or I'll nev - er

C7+5 C9 Fm7 B♭9 E♭

fall in love. In a rest - less world like

B♭7♭9 E♭ B♭m C9

this is, love is end - ed be - fore it's be - gun, And too

Fm7 C7♭9 Fm Fm7

man - y moon - light kiss - es seem to cool in the warmth of the

Fm7/B♭
B♭9
E♭
E♭
C7♭9
Fm7
B♭7♭9
sun. When I give my heart it will be com - plete-ly,
E♭
C7+5
C7
Fm7
B♭9
E♭
or I'll nev - er give my heart, And the mo - ment I can
A♭
C7+5
C7
C7+5
Fm
A♭m6
E♭
C7♭9
feel that you feel that way too, is when I fall in
1
2
Fm7
B♭7
E♭6
C9
Fm7
B♭7♭9
E♭6
Fm7
B♭7♭9
E♭maj7
love with you. you.
rit.

UNFORGETTABLE

Words and Music by
IRVING GORDON

G
Gdim
UN-FOR-GET-TA-BLE, in ev-'ry way,
C
A9
Em7
And for-ev-er-more, that's how you'll stay.
Cm
A9
F
Fm
C
Gm6
That's why, dar-ling, it's in-cred-i-ble, That some-one so
A7
D7
G7
UN-FOR-GET-TA-BLE Thinks that I am UN-FOR-GET-TA-BLE,
1.
C
C#7
D7
C#7
Am7
D7
2
C
Dm7
Db7
C6
too.
too.
mf

MONA LISA

Words and Music by
JAY LIVINGSTON and
RAY EVANS

Refrain Slowly Rubato
Eb
Ab
Eb
Mo - na Li - sa, Mo - na Li - sa men have named you: You're so
mp
mf
Fm7
Bb7
Fm
like the la - dy with the mys - tic smile. Is it on - ly 'cause you're lone - ly_ they have
mp
Bb7
Eb
blamed you for that Mo - na Li - sa strange - ness in your smile? Do you
Ab
Eb
smile to tempt a lov - er,_ Mo - na Li - sa,_ Or is
mf

Ab Abm

this your way to hide a brok-en heart? Man-y dreams have been brought to your

mp

Eb Bb7 Eb Eb7

door - step. They just lie there, and they die there. Are you

Ab Eb

warm, are you real, Mo - na Li - sa, Or just a

Bb7 1. Eb 2. Eb

cold and lone-ly, love-ly work of art? Mo - na art?

rall.

THOSE LAZY-HAZY-CRAZY DAYS OF SUMMER

Words by
CHARLES TOBIAS

Music by
HANS CARSTE

E7
1. Just fill your bas-ket full of sand-wich-es and ween-ies, Then lock the
2. Don't have to tell a girl and fel-ler 'bout a drive-in, Or some ro-
3. And there's the good old fash-ioned pic-nic, and they still go, Al-ways
Am
D7
house up Now you're set. And on the beach you'll see the
man-tic mov-ie scene. Why, from the mo-ment that those
will go an-y time. And there will al-ways be a
Am7
Fdim
D7
girls in their bi-ki-nis. As cute as ev-er but they
lov-ers start ar-riv-in', You'll see more kiss-ing in the
mo-ment that can thrill so, As when the old quar-tette sings
G7
C
Cdim
G7
C
nev-er get 'em wet.
cars than on the screen.
out, "Sweet A-del-ine."
Roll out Those La-zy-Ha-zy-

D7
G7
Cra - zy Days Of Sum - mer; Those days of so - da and
Dm7
G7
C
Cdim
G7
C
pret - zels and beer. Roll out Those La - zy - Ha - zy -
D7
G7
Cra - zy Days Of Sum - mer; You'll wish that sum - mer could
Dm7
G7
1.C
Cdim
G7
2.C
al - ways be here. Roll out Those here.
8

SWEET LORRAINE

Words by
MITCHELL PARISH

Music by
CLIFF BURWELL

Em
A7/E
A7
D7
Gee, but I feel proud, want to shout right out loud:
Can't wait till the day, when I'll take her a - way:
Chorus
Slowly
D7(♯5)
G
E7
A7
D7
Em
C7
B7
E7
A7
I've just found joy, I'm as hap-py as a ba-by boy With an-oth-er brand new choo-choo toy,
mp-f
D7
G
Am7
D7
D7(♯5)
G
E7
A7
D7
When I'm with my sweet Lor - raine; A pair of eyes That are blu-er than the
Em
C7
B7
E7
A7
D7
G
summer skies When you see them you will re - a - lize Why I love my sweet Lor-raine,

G7 C E7/B Am C7/G F E7 Am C7/G
(I'm so hap-py,) When it's rain-ing I don't miss the sun, For it's in my sweet-ie's smile,
F7 E7 A7/Eb D7 F7 E7 A7 D7(#5)
Just to think that I'm the luck-y one Who will lead her down the aisle; Each
G E7 A7 D7 Em C7 B7 E7 A7
night I pray That no-bod-y steals her heart a-way, Just can't wait un-til that hap-py day,
1 2
D7 G A7 D7 G D7(#5) G
When I mar-ry sweet Lor-raine. I've -raine.
fz

NATURE BOY

Words and Music by
EDEN AHBEZ

Nature Boy - 3 - 1

G♯m7
Bdim (F♯bass)
Em7 (C♯bass)
F♯m7
A7
D7(sus)
B7(sus)
and sad of eye,
But
G♯7-9
G♯9
Gdim (G♯bass)
C♯9(sus)
ver - y wise
was
he.
F♯m9
G♯m7-5
F♯m9
And then one day,
one sum-mer day, he
passed my way
B7(F♯bass)
Bm6
F♯m7
B9
And as we spoke of
man - y things,
fools and kings,

Bm6
C♯7(sus)
D7
C♯7(sus)
D♯7
G♯m7
D7
This he said to me: "The great - est thing
G♯m7
Bdim (F♯bass)
Em7 (C♯bass)
F♯m7
A7
D7(sus)
B7(sus)
you'll ev - er learn Is
1.
G♯7-9
G♯7(sus)
Cdim/C♯
C♯7-9(sus)
F♯m9
G♯m7
C♯7-9
just to love and be loved in re - turn". There
2.
G♯7-9
C♯7-9
F♯m6 (add 9)
just to love and be loved in re - turn".

RAMBLIN' ROSE

Words and Music by
NOEL SHERMAN & JOE SHERMAN

Ramblin' Rose - 2 - 1

G7
Dm7
G7
C7
— no one knows Wild and
— days are gone Who will
— Heav - en knows Tho' I
F
C
wind - blown that's how you've grown,
love you with a love true,
love you with a love true,
Dm7
last time optional
G7sus
G7
— Who can cling to a Ram - blin'
— When your ram - blin' days are
— Who can cling to a Ram - blin'
C
F6
C
Ebdim
C
F6
C
1.2.
3. Fine
Rose? 2. Ram - ble
gone? 3. Ram - blin' Rose?

ANSWER ME
(My Love)

Words and Music by
WINKLER, RAUCH, SIGMAN

Ab6
Eb
Ebdim
Fm7
Bb7
Eb
Won't you tell me where I've gone a-stray? Please AN-SWER ME, MY LOVE.
Gm
Eb7
Gm
If you're hap-pi-er with-out me, I'll try not to care,
Ebm6
F7
Bb7
But if you still think a-bout me, Please lis-ten to my prayer.
Eb
Bb
Ab
Abm
Eb
You must know I've been true, Won't you say that we can start a-new,
Ab6
Eb
Ebdim
Fm7
Bb7
1 Eb Bb7
2 Eb
In my sor-row now I turn to you, Please AN-SWER ME, MY LOVE. LOVE.

AUTUMN LEAVES
(Les Feuilles Mortes)

French Lyric by JACQUES PREVERT
English Lyric by JOHNNY MERCER

Music by
JOSEPH KOSMA

Autumn Leaves - 2 - 1

F#m7-5
B7
Em
Tacet
Am7
D7
Gmaj7
C
G
miss you most of all my dar - ling, When Au - tumn Leaves start to fall. C'est une chan -
son, Qui nous res - sem - ble, Toi tu m'ai - mois Et je t'ai mais. Nous vi - vions
tous, Les deux en - sem - ble. Toi qui m'ai - mais Moi qui t'ai - mais. Mais la
vie sé - pare Ceux qui s'ai - ment Tout dou - ce - ment Sans faire de bruit. Et la
mer ef - fa - ce sur le sa - ble Les pas des a - mants dé - su - nis.
rit.

THE CHRISTMAS SONG
(Chestnuts Roasting On An Open Fire)

Music and Lyric by
MEL TORME & ROBERT WELLS

Cm Cm7 Abm6 Eb Am7 D7 Gm7 C7 Fm7 Bb7 Eb6
Ti - ny tots with their eyes all a - glow Will find it hard to sleep to - night. They know that
Bbm7 Eb9 Bbm7 Eb9 Bbm7 Eb9 Ab
San - ta's on his way; He's load-ed lots of toys and good-ies on his sleigh And ev - 'ry
Abm7 Db9 Gb Cm7 F7 Bb7
moth-er's child is gon-na spy To see if rein-deer real-ly know how to fly. And
Eb6 Bb7 Eb6 Bb9 Eb6 Eb9 Ab Ab7 G7+5
so, I'm of-fer-ing this sim - ple phrase To kids from one to nine-ty - two. Al -
Cm Cm7 Abm6 Eb Cm7 A7sus Ab7 Eb Cm7 Fm7 Bb7-9 Eb Bb11 Bb13-9 Eb6
tho' it's been said ma-ny times, ma-ny ways; "Mer-ry Christ-mas to you." you."
rit.
f
p

A BLOSSOM FELL

Cm7 F7 Cm7 F7 F7+ B♭ B♭7+
soon I saw you kiss-ing some-one new be-neath the moon I thought you
E♭ B♭ Cm7 F7
loved me You said you loved me We planned to-geth-er To dream for-
B♭dim B♭ B♭7+ E♭ E♭m B♭ B♭dim
ev - er The dream has end - ed For true love died The night A
Cm7 Fdim F7 B♭ B♮dim F7 B♭ E♭m B♭
Blos-som Fell and touched two lips that lied. A Blos-som lied.
1. 2.
rit.

CALYPSO BLUES

Words by
DON GEORGE

*Use A minor chord for entire song

Music by
NAT "KING" COLE

Sit - tin' by de o - cean me heart she feel so_ sad, ______ Don'
_ got de mon - ey to take me back to Trin - i - dad, ______
Fine cal - yp - so wo - man she cook me shrimp an'_ rice. ______
Fine cal - yp - so wo - man she cook me shrimp an'_ rice, ______ Dese

yon-kee hot dog don' treat me stom-ach ver-y nice.
In Trin-i-dad one dol-lar buy pa-
pay-a juice, ba-nan-a pie, six co-co-nut, one fe-male goat, an'
plen-ty fish to fill de boat; one bush-el bread, one bar-rel wine, an'
mf
mp

all de town she come to dine, but here is bad one dol - lar buy
cup of cof - fee, ham on rye.
Me
Me
throat she sick from neck - tie me feet she hurt from shoes me
hand she green from wrist - watch me o - ver - coat I lose me
pock - et full of emp - ty I got Cal - yp - so Blues.
heart she's full of lone - ly I got Cal - yp - so Blues.

Dese yon-kee girl give me big scare is
mf
mp
black de root, is blond de hair, her eye-lash false, her face is paint 'an
pads are where de girl she ain't; She jit-ter-bug when she should waltz, I
e - ven think her name is false bul cal - yp - so girl is
good a lot,_ is what you see_ is what she got.

Sit-tin' by de o-cean me heart she feel so_ sad,
Sit-tin' by de o-cean me heart she feel so_ sad.
Don'
_ got de mon-ey to take me back to Trin-i-dad.
Chant:
Wa-oo-oo wa-oo_ oo-wa-oo-wa-oo-wa-oo wa-ay
Wa-oo-oo wa-oo_ oo-wa-oo-wa oo-wa-oo wa-ay.
Die away

DARLING, JE VOUS AIME BEAUCOUP

Words and Music by
ANNA SOSENKO

Bb Bbm F
Ah, Cher - ie! my love for you is très, très fort;
mp
Dm A7 Dm7 G9 C7
Wish my French were good e - nough, I'd tell you So much more.
ten.
F Gm F Gm F7 Bb Bbm F Bdim G7 C7
But I hope that you com-pree All the things you mean to me. Dar-ling, je vous
p
F C9 F C7+
1.
aime beau-coup, I love you!
F C9 F C9 F
2.
aime beau-coup, I love you, yes, I do.
mf

I REMEMBER YOU

Words by
JOHNNY MERCER

Music by
VICTOR SCHERTZINGER

Refrain-Moderato, Not Too Fast, Expressively
G F♯7 G F G7sus G7
I re-mem-ber you. You're the one who made my dreams come
mp
Cmaj7 C6 Cm D7-9 G D7sus D7 D9 G
true a few kiss-es a-go. I re-mem-ber
F♯7 G F G7sus G7 Cmaj7 C Cm D7-9
you. You're the one who said: "I love you, too." I do. Did-n't you
G Dm7 G9 G7♭9 C F♯7 B7 E
know? I re-mem-ber too a dis-tant bell
mf

B7sus B7 Emaj7 E6 Em7 A7 Dmaj7 D6 D7
and stars that fell like rain, out of the blue.
mf dim. poco a poco
p
G F♯7 G Bm7-5 E7-9 Am
When my life is through and the an-gels ask me to re-call
mp
f dim. poco a poco
Cm Cm6 G A9 G C♯°
the thrill of them all, then I shall tell them I re-
mp
Am7 D7-9 G A9 D7 D7-9 D9 D7-8 G A7-9 D9 addB G
mem-ber you. you.
mf
rall.

LET THERE BE LOVE

Words by
IAN GRANT

Music by
LIONEL RAND

Eb
Ebm
Ebdim
Fm7
rain
Chi - le con car - ne
Bb7
Eb
Eb
And spark-ling cham - pagne
Let there be birds
Gm
Bbm6
C7
Abm6
To sing in the trees
Some-one to bless me

Bb7
Eb
Bb7
Eb
Whenever I sneeze
Let there be
Eb
Gm7
Bbm6
C9
cuckoos,
A lark and a dove
C7
Fm7
Bb7
But first of all, please
LET THERE BE
1 Eb
Ebdim
Fm7
Bb7
2 Eb
Abm6
Eb6
LOVE.
Let there be
LOVE.
pp

IT'S ONLY A PAPER MOON

Words by
BILLY ROSE & E.Y. HARBURG

Music by
HAROLD ARLEN

G
Edim
Am7
D7
G
E9
mm, A bub - ble for a min - ute, Mm,
A9
D7
G
Am7
A7
Am7
D+
mm, You smile, the bub-ble has a rain-bow in it.
rit
Chorus
G
Ddim
Am7
D7
Am7
D9
Say, it's on-ly a pa-per moon, Sail-ing o-ver a
mf a tempo
G
D7
G
Dm
Am7
card-board sea, But it would-n't be make be-lieve, If you

D7 Am7 D7 G Eb7 Am6 G Ddim
be - lieved in me. Yes, it's on - ly a
Am7 D7 Am7 D9 G D7 G
can - vas sky, Hang - ing o - ver a mus - lin tree,
Dm Am7 D7 Am7 D7
But it would - n't be make be - lieve, If you be - lieved in me.
G C6 Cm7 Gmaj7 Am7 D7
With - out your love, it's a hon - ky - tonk pa -

G
C6
Cm7
Gmaj7
rade, With - out your love, it's a
G
Dm
E7
A9
D7+5
G
Ddim
mel- o - dy played in a pen - ny ar - cade. It's a Bar - num and
Am7
D7
Am7
D9
G
Dm
Bai - ley world, Just as phon - y as it can be, But it would - n't be
Am7
D7
Am7
D7
1. G
Am7
D7
2. G
make be - lieve If you be - lieved in me.

LOVE IS THE THING
Lyric by
NED WASHINGTON
Music by
VICTOR YOUNG
Slow
mf
p
VOICE
Fm G7 C Fm G7
My dar - ling, all a - round us peo - ple clam - or, They're striv - ing for the things they'll nev - er
mp
C Em Am B7 Em G C D7 G7 Gaug
own, The on - ly thing that has - n't lost its glam - our Is love and love a - lone.
rit.
CHORUS
C Am F G7 C Cdim Dm G7
What does it mat - ter if we're rich or we're poor? For - tune and fame, They nev - er en - dure, Oh,
mp-mf
C Em Edim G7 Gaug C Em Edim F Em G7 C Am
love is the thing, Love is the thing! What good is mon - ey if your
Love Is The Thing - 2 - 1

F G7 C Cdim Dm G7 C Em Edim G7 B7
heart is-n't light? Here in your arms, I'm wealth-y to-night, When youth has its fling, Love is the
E F Fm C
thing! While oth-ers fight for pow'r, We can walk a-mong the flow'rs,
Cdim F G7 Gaug C Edim F G7
Know-ing that the best thing in life is a thing that's free, Love for you and me,
F G7 C Cdim Dm G7
And ev-en tho' our cast-les crum-ble and fall, We have the right to laugh at them all, For
C Em Edim G7 Gaug rit. 1. C D7 G7 Gaug G7 2. C Ab7 Gb7 C
love is still King, Love is the thing! thing!
rit.
p
molto rit.
pp

LOVE LETTERS

Words by
EDWARD HEYMAN

Music by
VICTOR YOUNG

G
Em
A♯dim
F♯7
Bm
Dm
E7
part
I'm not a - lone in the night
Am
G♯dim
E7
Am
Cm
D7
G
When I can have all the love you write.
I mem-o-
Em
Am
F♯dim
rize ev-'ry line
I kiss the name that you
G7
G9
Bdim
C
Cm
D7
G
C♯dim
sign
And, dar-ling, then I read a - gain right from the start
Am7
F♯dim
1 G
C♯dim
Am7
D7
2 G
C
G
Love let - ters straight from your heart.
heart.

LUSH LIFE

Words and Music by
BILLY STRAYHORN

Abm7 D7/A Db6/9 D9 Db6/9 C7(#5) Fm Fm6
washed a-way by too man-y through the day twelve o' clock tales Then you came a-long with
Fm7 Fm6 Gm7 C7(b9) Fm Fm6
your si-ren song to tempt me to mad-ness I thought for a while that
Fm7 Fm6 Bbm/F C7(b9)/Fb Ebm7 A13 B9(b5)
your poiq-nant smile was tinged with the sad-ness of a great love for me
Bb7(b9) Ebm7 A9(b5) Ebm7/Ab Ab13(b9)
Ah! yes I was wrong a-gain I was wrong
Chorus
Db D6 Db D Db6 C9(b5) E Eb D
Life is lone-ly a-gain and on-ly last year ev-ry thing seemed so sure Now

Db D6 Db D Db6 Db7 C7 F E Eb
life is aw-ful a - gain a trough-ful of hearts could on-ly be a bore A
Ab6 Eb7(#5) Ab6/Eb Em9 A7(b9) D C B Bb13 A13 Ab13
week in Pa-ris will ease the bite of it All I care is to smile in spite of it
Db D6 Db D Db6 C7(b5) B7(b9) Bb7(b9)
I'll for-get you I will while yet you are still burn-ing in-side my brain Ro-
Ebm9 Gbm9 A7(#5) Ab7 Dbmaj7 Dbm9 Gb7(b9) Cbmaj7 Bb7(b9)/D
mance is mush sti-fling those who strive I'll live a LUSH LIFE in some small dive And
Gbmaj7 Gb9 A7(#5) Ab13 E Eb6 Dmaj7 G7 Dbmaj7
there I'll be, while I rot with the rest of those whose lives are lone-ly too.

MOON LOVE

Words and Music by
MACK DAVID, MACK DAVIS
& ANDRE KOSTELANETZ

Refrain
a tempo
Bb7
Bb7/Ab
Eb/G
Eb
Will this be moon love nothing but moon love? Will you be
mp-mf a tempo
Fm7
Bb7
Eb
Eb/G
gone when the dawn comes steal - ing through? Are these just
Bb7
Bb7/Ab
Eb/G
Eb
moon dreams Grand while the moon beams? But when the
F9/C
D7
Gm
Gm7(b5)/F
C7/E
moon fades a - way will my dreams come true? Much as I love you

Fm7 Bb7/D Eb F9/C Eb/Bb

Don't let me love you If I must pay for your

F9/A Bb7/Ab Eb/G Cm7 Bb7

kiss with lone - ly tears. Say it's not moon love

Bb7/Ab Eb/G Eb Cm7 F7

Tell me it's true love Say you'll be mine when the

Fm9/Bb Bb7 1. Eb Bb7 2. Eb Abmaj7 Eb

moon dis - ap - pears. Will this be pears.

rit.

RED SAILS IN THE SUNSET

Words by
JIMMY KENNEDY

Music by
HUGH WILLIAMS

Slowly (with expression) ♩ = 88

mf

G D7 G D G7 C G+ Cm6

mp

Red Sails In The Sun - set 'Way out on the

G G♯dim D7 G♯dim Am7 D7

sea, Oh! car-ry my loved one

Am7 D7 G D7+ G

Home safe - ly to me. He sailed at the

mp

D7
G
D
G7
C
G+
Cm6
G
G♯dim
dawn - ing
All day I've - been blue
D7
G♯dim
Am7
D7
Am7
D7
Red Sails In The Sun - set,
I'm trust - ing in
G
Dm7
G7
C
Cm
G
D7
C7
you.
Swift wings you must bor - row
Make straight for the
G
Dm7
G7
C
Cm
G
shore
We mar - ry to - mor - row

A7
Am7
D9
G
D7
G
D
G7
And he goes sail-ing no more
Red Sail In The Sun-set
poco rit.
mp
C
G+
Cm6
G
G♯dim
D7
G♯dim
'Way out on the sea
Oh! car-ry my
Am7
D7
Am7
D7
1 G
G♯dim
Am7
D7
loved one
Home safe-ly to me.
2 G
G7
C
Cm6
G♭
G6
me.
accel.
dim.
poco rit.
pp

STRAIGHTEN UP AND FLY RIGHT

Words and Music by
NAT "KING" COLE
and IRVING MILLS

Straighten Up And Fly Right - 3 - 1

A♭6
D♭6
B♭m7
E♭9
E9
Fm
E♭7
C7
STRAIGH-TEN UP AND FLY_ RIGHT!_ STRAIGH-TEN UP AND FLY_ RIGHT!_
STRAIGH-TEN UP AND FLY_ RIGHT!_ Cool down Pa-pa, don't you blow your top._
Ain't no use in div - in',_ What's the use in div - in'?_ STRAIGH-TEN UP AND FLY
_ RIGHT,_ Cool_down, Pa-pa, don't you blow your top._ The buz-zard told the mon-key, "You are
mp-f
fz
fz

F7
F9
G♭9
F9
B♭9
chok-in' me, Re-lease your holt and I will set you free," The mon-key looked the buz-zard right
B♭9
B♭7
E♭9
B♭m7
E9
E♭9
dead in the eye, And said, "Your sto-ry's so touch-ing, it sounds just like a lie."
fz
A♭6
D♭6
A♭6
B♭m7
E♭9
STRAIGH-TEN UP AND FLY RIGHT! Straigh-ten up and stay right.
fz fz
fz fz
A♭6
D♭6
A♭6
Fm
E♭9
E♭7
A♭6
E♭+
E♭9
E♭7
A♭6
1
2
STRAIGH-TEN UP AND FLY RIGHT! Cool down, Pa-pa, don't you blow your top. blow your top.
fz
fz

TANGERINE

Words by
JOHNNY MERCER

Music by
VICTOR SCHERTZINGER

D7+
Gm7
Eb
C7
F
Abdim
Refrain
mp-mf
Tan - ge rine
She is all they claim
With her
eyes of night and lips as bright as flame
Tan - ge -
rine
When she danc - es by
Sen - or - i - tas stare and
E7
G♯dim
A
F♯m
ca - bal - le - ros sigh.
Bm7
E9
A7
A+
D7
And I've seen

C7
F
Abdim
Gm7
C7
Toasts to Tan - ge - rine
Raised in ev - 'ry bar a -
Gm7
C7
A7
A+
D
D7+
D7
Gm
cross the Ar - gen - tine,
Yes, she has them all on the
dim. poco a poco - -
A7sus
A7
Dm7
F
G7
Bbm
Bb
Gm7
run But her heart be - longs to just one Her heart be - longs to
p-mp
C7
F
Cm
D7
D7+
F
Bb
F
Tan - ge - rine. Tan - ge - rine.
rit.
ppp

TONIGHT YOU BELONG TO ME

By
BILLY ROSE and LEE DAVID

Cm
F
Cm7
F6
B♭7
will, You have the same old ap - peal.
side, Don't close the door on your dreams.
Chorus
E♭
E♭7
A♭
A♭m
E♭
Though you be - long to some - bod - y else, To - night you be -
p - f
B♭7
E♭
B♭7
E♭
E♭7
long to me. Though we're a - part, you're
A♭
A♭m
E♭
B♭7
E♭
part of my heart, To - night you be - long to me.

Abm
Down by the stream, how sweet it will seem,
sfz
Eb
Eb7/Db
C7
Fm7
Bb7
Eb
Once more to dream in the moon - light.
Though with the
Eb7
Ab
Abm
Eb
Bb7
dawn, I know you'll be gone, To - night you be - long to
L.H.
1
Eb
Abm
Bbaug
me!
2
Eb
me!

(Get Your Kicks On) ROUTE 66!

Words and Music by
BOBBY TROUP

Gm7 C7 F Bb9 F
Now you go thru Saint Loo-ey and Jop-lin, Mis-sour-i And Ok-la-hom-a Cit-y is might-
F9 F7 Bb9 F
-y pret-ty; You'll see Am-ar-il-lo; Gal-lup, New
Fdim F Gm7 C9 Gm7 C9 F F#dim
Mex-i-co; Flag-staff, Ar-i-zon-a; Don't for-get Wi-no-na, King-man, Bar-stow,
Gm7 C7 F Bb9 E F
San Ber-nar-din-o Won't you get hip to this time-ly tip:
Bb9 F
When you make that Cal-i-for-nia trip Get your
Gm7 C9 C7 F Abdim Gm7 C7 F Bb9 F Gb7 F
kicks on ROUTE SIX-TY-SIX! If
mf
f
2

STAR DUST

Words by
MITCHELL PARISH
French translation by Yvette Baruch

Music by
HOAGY CARMICHAEL

G7 Gdim G7 C7+5 F6 Fm6
song. Be - side a gar - den wall, when stars are bright,
son. E - toile du soir brill - ant, é - toile d' amour,
C Em A7
you are in my arms, The night - in - gale tells his fair - y tale
Tu es dans mes bras, Le ros - si - gnole chante et puis s'en - vole
Dm7 A7 Dm7 Fm6 Dm7-5 Fm
of par - a - dise, where ros - es grew. Tho' I dream in vain. In my
au pa - ra - dis des âmes ra - vies. Donc mon rêve s'en - fuit, Comme une
C G Am C B7 B7-5 E7 E7+5 F6 A7 Adim G7
heart it will re - main: My star dust mel - o - dy, The mem - o - ry of love's re -
chan - son dans la nuit Et mon é - toile d'a - mour N'est qu'une mé - moire d'une mél - o -
1. C Ab7 Fm6 G7 C7+5 2. C C6 Cm Cmaj7 C6
frain. Some - times I frain.
die. Sou - vent le die.
l.h.

SMILE

Words and Music by
TURNER, PARSONS, CHAPLIN

F
Light up your face witn glad-ness, Hide ev-'ry trace of sad ness,
Fdim
Gm
Adim
Gm
D7-9
Gm
D7
Al - tho' a tear may be ev - er so near, That's the
Gm
B♭m
E♭9
time you must keep on try - ing, SMILE, what's the use of cry - ing,
F
Gm
C7
You'll find that life is still worth while, If you'll just
1.
F
Gm7
C9
C7-9
SMILE.
2.
F
Fmaj7
F6
SMILE.
rall.

THAT'S MY GIRL

Words by
BARBARA TOBIAS

Music by
RAY ELLINGTON

F9♯5
F7
B♭6
Cm7
B♭6
F7♯5
B♭6
F9
e - ven her name. 'Cause That's My Girl! I'm add - ing her to my fam - i - ly.
B♭6
Fm7
B♭9
Fm7
B♭7
E♭
And I love that girl and ev - 'ry - thing's fine.
E♭6
Edim
So un - til the day that she says "Yes" I'm
B♭
Dm7
G9
G7
Cm7
F7
keep - ing my fin - gers crossed. 'Cause That's My Girl! And she's gon - na stay
B♭
Cm7
F♯7
F9
B♭
Cm7
B7
B♭maj9
mine.
mine.

THESE FOOLISH THINGS

(Remind Me Of You)

Words and Music by
MARVELL, STRACHEY, LINK

B♭ mi
E♭ 7
F mi
C mi
F 7
B♭ 7
And still those lit-tle things re- main,
That bring me hap-pi-ness or pain.
rit.
CHORUS
E♭
C mi
F mi
B♭ 7
E♭
C mi
1. A cig-a-rette that bears a lip-stick's tra-ces,
An air-line tick-et to ro-
2. First daf-fo-dils and long ex-cit-ed ca-bles,
And can-dle lights on lit-tle
3. Gar-de-nia per-fume ling-'ring on a pil-low,
Wild straw-b'ries on-ly sev-en
R.H.
R.H.
F9
B♭ 7
E♭ 9
A♭
C7
man-tic pla-ces,
And still my heart has wings.
THESE FOOL-ISH
cor-ner ta-bles,
And still my heart has wings.
THESE FOOL-ISH
francs a ki-lo,
And still my heart has wings.
THESE FOOL-ISH

F9
F mi
Bb7
Eb
C mi
THINGS re-mind me of you. A tink-ling pia-no in the
THINGS re-mind me of you. The park at eve-ning when the
THINGS re-mind me of you. The smile of Gar-bo and the
R.H.
F mi
Bb7
Eb
C mi
F9
Bb7
next a-part-ment, Those stumb-ling words that told you what my heart meant,
bell has sound-ed, The "Ile de France" with all the gulls a-round it,
scent of ro-ses, The wait-ers whist-ling as the last bar clo-ses,
R.H.
Eb9
Ab
C7
F9
Bb7
A fair-ground's paint-ed swings, THESE FOOL-ISH THINGS re-mind me of
The beau-ty that is Spring's, THESE FOOL-ISH THINGS re-mind me of
The song that Cros-by sings, THESE FOOL-ISH THINGS re-mind me of
Eb
D7
G mi
C mi
D9
G mi
C9
you. You came, you saw, you con-quer'd me;
you. How strange, how sweet, to find you still;
you. How strange, how sweet, to find you still;

B♭ Gmi E♭ F7 B♭7 B♭dim. Fmi B♭7
When you did that to me, I knew some-how this had to be.
These things are dear to me, They seem to bring you near to me.
These things are dear to me, They seem to bring you near to me.
E♭ Cmi Fmi B♭7 E♭ Cmi
The winds of March that make my heart a danc-er, A tel-e-phone that rings but
The sigh of mid-night trains in emp-ty sta-tions, Silk stock-ings thrown a-side, dance
The scent of smould-'ring leaves, the wail of steam-ers, Two lov-ers on the street who
R.H.
F9 B♭7 E♭9 A♭ C7
who's to an-swer? Oh, how the ghost of you clings! THESE FOOL-ISH
in-vi-ta-tions. Oh, how the ghost of you clings! THESE FOOL-ISH
walk like dream-ers. Oh, how the ghost of you clings! THESE FOOL-ISH
F9 B♭7 E♭ B♭dim. Cmi B♭aug. E♭
1. 2.
THINGS re-mind me of you. you.
THINGS re-mind me of you. you.
THINGS re-mind me of you. you.
L.H.
Ped.

WHEN I TAKE MY SUGAR TO TEA

Gm7
Caug
F
Gm7
C7
D♭7
C7
F
on the cor - ner, For the moon in lov - er's lane;
C
G7
C7
I'm do - ing things I nev - er did be - fore:
REFRAIN
p - mf
F
Cdim
C7
F
Cdim
When I take my su-gar to tea, All the boys are jeal-ous of
C7
D7
Gm7
B♭m
me; 'Cause I nev - er take her where the gang goes, When I

F C7 F B♭ F C F Cdim C7
take my sug-ar to tea. I'm a row-dy dow-dy, that's me, She's a
F Cdim C7 D7
high-hat ba-by, That's she. So I nev-er take her where the
Gm7 B♭m F C7 F F7 Cdim B♭
gang goes, When I take my sug-ar to tea. Ev-'ry Sun-day
E♭7
af-ter-noon, We for-get a-bout our cares,

F
G7
D♭7
Rub - bing el - bows at the Ritz
With those mil - lion -
C7 Cdim C7
F
Cdim
C7
aires. When I take my sug - ar to tea, I'm as
F
Cdim
C7
D7
Ritz - y as I can be, 'Cause I nev - er take her where the
1.
2.
Gm7 B♭m
F
C7
F B♭ F C7
F
gang goes, When I take my sug - ar to tea. When I tea.
sfz

WHERE CAN I GO WITHOUT YOU?

Words by
PEGGY LEE

Music by
VICTOR YOUNG

Where Can I Go Without You - 2 - 1

F G9 C7 F Cm7 F7
WHERE CAN I GO WITH - OUT YOU ? I want - ed trav- el, I want - ed
Bb Bbdim Cm7 F7 Bb Dm7 G7
ro - mance, I chased that rain - bow a - cross the sea; I'm tired of fac - es and quaint old
C Cdim Dm7 G7 Gm7 C7 F
plac - es, If you can't be there with me. Back on the boat a - gain and
Gm7 C7 F Dm7 Gm7 C9 F Faug
fare - well to France, Fare - well to Lon - don town, they have - n't a chance; I'll trade the sights I've seen, for
Bb6 Bbm6 F G9 C7 1. F Fdim Gm7 C7 2. F Eb9 F6
one lov - ing glance, WHERE CAN I GO WITH - OUT YOU ? YOU ?

TWILIGHT ON THE TRAIL

Words and Music by
SIDNEY D. MITCHELL
and LOUIS ALTER

Eb
Bb Eb
twi - light on the trail And I rest once more My
Ab
Gm Ab
Fm Ab Eb
ceil - ing is the sky, And the grass on which I lie Is my floor
Ab
Bb7 Ab
Abm Eb
Gm
Nev - er ev - er
C7
Ab7
Gm
have a nick - el in my jeans
Nev - er ev - er have a debt to
C7 Ab7
Gm
C7
pay,
Still I un - der - stand what real con - tent - ment means.

Ab7
Bb
Edim
F7
rit.
F7b5
Bb7
tempo
Guess I was born that way
When it's
a tempo
Eb
Bb
Eb
twi - light on the trail
And my voice is
Ab
Gm
Ab
Fm
Ab
still
Please plant this heart of mine
Un-der-neath the lone-some pine
on the
Eb
Ab
Bb7
Ab
Abm
1. Eb
Bb7
hill.
l.h.
When it's
2. Eb
Eb
Coda Optional
Ab
Eb
Abm
Eb
When it's twi- light on the trail.
l.h.
p
pp

YES! WE HAVE NO BANANAS

By
FRANK SILVER and
IRVING COHN

G
D
G7
He just "yes - ses" you to death And as he takes your dough- he tells you:
Some one asked for 'Spar - row - grass' And then the whole quar - tette- all ans-wered:
Chorus
C
F
C/E
G7
C
D7
YES! We have no ba - na - nas We have no ba -
pf
G7
C
F
Fm6
na - nas to - day We've string beans and HON-ions, cab -
C/G
B7
E
BAH - ges and scal - lions And all kinds of fruit and say

G7
C
F
C
We have an old fashion-ioned to-MAH-to
F
G7
C
Long Is-land po-TAH-to But YES! we
F
C/E
G7
C
A7
D7
G7
have no ba-na-nas We have no ba-na-nas to-
C
D7
G7
C
1
2
day.
day

EXIT